Look What

Can Do!

BIOGRAPHIES OF MISSION HEROES

Jess Jennings

ACKNOWLEDGMENTS

A book is seldom ever written alone. *Look What God Can Do* is no exception. All the information in this volume originated from many sources as indicated in the bibliography. These authors did the hard work of original research and now with the help of many, their work will be presented to a new generation.

I appreciate Lyra G. Villarante and the other members of the CSM team for the cover design, formatting, and the many details involved with helping print this book. *Nehemiah Teams* 2004-2006 have read this book in their heart language and responded enthusiastically as they learned about these heroes of the past, therefore, I thank these many young people for their encouragement to continue this project. Most of all, I thank Wendy, for her continued love and encouragement.

DEDICATION

*To Wendy, David,
Krysten, and Betsy*

TABLE OF CONTENTS

INTRODUCTION

D. L. Moody was the greatest evangelist of the nineteenth century. He preached to more people than anyone ever had up to that point in history. Thousands upon thousands gave their lives to Christ after hearing Moody preach! What was it that made Moody great? It wasn't his speaking ability or his educational level. Moody never finished elementary school, and it was reported that in his preaching, he made many grammatical errors.

Also his greatness was not because of his personality or looks. He was rather ordinary, both in personality and his physical appearance. What then was his secret? Why was the gospel so powerfully advanced through the life and preaching of D. L. Moody?

When Moody was a young man, he was challenged by these words, "The world has yet to see what God can do through one person totally surrendered to Him." Moody responded, "By the grace of God, I will be that person." D. L. Moody was great because he was surrendered to the Lordship of Jesus Christ.

Bill Bright, founder of Campus Crusade for Christ, has been the instrument by which the gospel has been presented to over three billion people in the last thirty years through such tools as the *Jesus* film and gospel tracts.

Campus Crusade has several thousand missionaries working in almost every country in the world. Someone once asked Bill Bright why God had used him in such a big way. Bill replied, "When I was young, I wrote a letter to God which stated, 'I, Bill Bright, from this day forward am a slave of Jesus Christ,' then I signed my name."

This book has been written to introduce you, the reader, to some ordinary people who impacted and influenced their generation for Christ. My prayer is that you will be challenged, changed, and inspired by these short biographies, but most importantly, that you will be led to finish the task of reaching every people group with the gospel of Jesus Christ in this generation.

The world *has* seen what God can do through individuals totally surrendered to Him. The world *has yet* to see what God can do through you.

Jess Jennings

PATRICK OF IRELAND
(389-469(?))

Patrick, born in 389, is probably the best-known fifth century missionary. He was born into a Christian home in the Roman province of Britain, but did not receive the Lord until he was in his late teens. His life, much like the biblical character Joseph, was tested and shaped by severe trials. When Patrick was sixteen, he was captured by a band of pirates and taken to the country of Ireland. He was sold as a slave to a local farmer, where for the next six years he took care of cattle and pigs.

This time of captivity however was not wasted. Patrick records that he began to think about his spiritual condition. It was during this time that his life changed. He records, "The Lord opened the understanding of my unbelief, that, late as it was, I might remember my faults and turn to the Lord my God with all my heart; and He had regard to my low estate, and pitied my youth and ignorance, and kept guard over me even before I knew him, and before I attained wisdom to distinguish good from evil; and he strengthened and comforted me as a father does his son." (Tucker, p. 38)

After several years, Patrick was freed and boarded a ship for Britain. As the ship left the Irish harbor, many thoughts must have come to his mind. Why had this happened to him? Would his family still be alive? What joy there must have been to leave this place for good and never return. Only later would he see God's purpose and plan.

The trip would not take long, so he thought. However, his ship was blown off course by a storm and landed in Gaul. Patrick was again taken as a slave. I'm sure it seemed his hard times would never end. He turned to the only one who could help him, his heavenly Father. Patrick had learned the discipline of praying without giving up. Prayer, to him, was talking with a God who loved him. During these times of prayer, he began to know and understand God's voice speaking to him. On one such occasion this "inner voice" told him to go to the seacoast, where he would find a ship to take him away. Sure enough, it was as he had been told. He escaped and returned to his family in Britain.

He could now continue on with his life, so he thought. However, not long after his return to Britain, God spoke to Patrick through a vision similar to the apostle Paul's calling to Macedonia, recorded in Acts chapter 16. Patrick relates that, "I saw a man named Victoricus, coming as if from Ireland, with innumerable letters; and he gave me one of these, and ...while I was reading the beginning of the letter, I thought that at that very moment I heard a voice of those who were beside the wood of Focluth, near the western sea; and this is what they called out: 'Please, holy boy, come and walk among us again.' Their cry pierced to my very heart, and I could read no more; and so I awoke." (Tucker, p. 39)

After his dramatic call, Patrick began to prepare himself by involvement in a local church and was ordained as a deacon. He knew that if God had called, then he must prepare. He also knew that if God had called him, then God would make a way for him to go back to Ireland. Patrick's superiors doubted his ability for such a mission and denied his request to be sent back to Ireland. Another was sent in his place, but died in less than a year after his arrival in Ireland, opening the door for Patrick. Even though Patrick was now over forty, God had opened a way for him to go. Patrick was now ready! Church leaders had assumed his age was a barrier, but God had taken his time shaping Patrick's character for such a huge task.

Twenty-five years had passed since Patrick had made his first voyage to Ireland. The first trip was a trip of remorse and bitterness. The second trip was full of joy and purpose. He had gone the first time as a slave both spiritually and physically. He was returning as a free man with a gospel of power and hope.

Patrick was probably not the first to preach in Ireland. It is recorded that upon his arrival there in 432, there were small groups of Christians already meeting. Other Christians, no doubt had been taken as captives to Ireland, and some Christian traders had done business there. Nevertheless, much of Ireland was not evangelized and had much paganism. They worshiped the sun, moon, rocks, wind, and fire, and believed that many spirits lived in the trees, hills, and rivers and creeks. Animism is another name for this kind of belief system. There were many witchdoctors who were the mediators between man and these many spirits. Animal as well and human sacrifices were a regular part of appeasing the spirits. The people, no doubt, wore different kinds of amulets to protect them from evil spirits.

Patrick was met by immediate opposition, but won many people to Christ by what today is termed as a "power encounter." Miracles done in the name of Jesus were what convinced the people to believe. Many tribal chiefs were won to Christ when they saw the power of the gospel, and within a short time after Patrick's arrival, the king granted religious toleration for Christians in Ireland. Scripture testifies that this display of God's power was also a pattern for evangelism in the apostles' ministry. In Acts 13, as Paul and Barnabas entered Paphos, they were met and opposed by a sorcerer named Bar-Jesus. Paul, filled with the Holy Spirit, looked straight at the man and said, "*You are a child of the devil and an enemy of everything that is right! Now the hand of the Lord is against you. You are going to be blind, and for a time you will be unable to see the light of the sun. Immediately mist and darkness came over him and he was unable to see.*" As a result of this miracle, the governor became a believer (Acts 13:6-12).

Patrick's method of evangelism was to try and win the political leaders in hopes that those under them would follow suit. In using this method, he may have been thinking about Cornelius, who gathered all his family and friends together to hear the gospel (Acts 10). Converts were then taught the Scriptures and were encouraged to become involved in ministry themselves.

For over thirty years, Patrick labored. He left his home, returned to the place of his captivity, and endured tremendous persecutions. Patrick records that twelve times he faced life-threatening situations, including a harrowing kidnapping and a two week captivity. Surely, at times, he must have been lonely and discouraged, but he continued until over two hundred churches were established and an estimated one hundred thousand converts were baptized. Patrick's concluding remarks give God the credit for any success. He said in effect, "Look what God has done."

COUNT NICOLAUS LUDWIG VON ZINZENDORF
(1700-1760)

"One of the greatest missionary leaders of all times and the individual who did the most to advance the cause of Protestant missions during the course of the eighteenth century was Count Nicolas Ludwig von Zinzendorf." (Tucker, p.69) He was born in 1700 into wealth and nobility. After the death of his father, his grandmother and aunt, who were both dedicated pietists, raised him.

Pietists were those who placed a great deal of emphasis on a personal relationship with Jesus Christ as Lord. This emphasis was in sharp contrast to the spiritual deadness and traditions of many in that day. Zinzendorf who came to know the Lord as his personal Savior at a very early age, made a commitment that "his lifelong purpose should be to preach the gospel of Jesus Christ throughout the world." (Howard, p.55)

While attending school from 1710-1716, he along with five others formed the Order of the Grain of Mustard Seed. This small group committed themselves to pray and purposed to do four things: To witness to the power of Jesus Christ, to draw other Christians together in fellowship, to help those who were suffering for their faith, and to carry the gospel of Christ to those overseas who had not yet heard the message. (Howard, p.55)

Zinzendorf longed to enter the Christian ministry, but for a nobleman, that would be unthinkable. He continued his studies in law to prepare for a career in working for the government, but was "very unhappy with this choice for his future." (Tucker, p.70) Zinzendorf might have continued in this direction had not God, in his grace stopped Zinzendorf and made His plans known. God has always been the initiator of bringing people into the center of His will. God is the one who pursues man. God is the one who speaks to those willing to listen. God had not forgotten Zinzendorf's commitment as a child or his commitment as a teenager in the Order of the Grain of Mustard Seed.

One of the ways in which God made his plan known to Zinzendorf was through a painting depicting Christ enduring the crown of thorns. Under the painting was an inscription which read, "All this I did for you, what are you doing for me?" On that day in 1719, Zinzendorf surrendered all to Christ. In that moment his life's purpose was set in motion. Like Abraham, who left for a land that God would show him, Zinzendorf began to walk in faith. God had not told him what he was supposed to do or where he was supposed to go. He had simply asked Zinzendorf the question, "What are you doing for me?"

For three years, Zinzendorf walked in the light in which God had given, waiting for the next revelation of His will. This next step came in a most unusual way, and was surely not recognized at first as being a part of God's plan to take the gospel around the world through Zinzendorf. In 1722, a group of Protestant refugees sought shelter in Zinzendorf's estate. Here they would be safe from persecution and could worship in freedom. His estate was quickly named "Herrnhut," meaning "the Lord's watch." As word spread of Zinzendorf's generosity, many other refugees sought refuge there until there was a thriving community. This community became known as the Moravian community. Even at this point, no one could have imagined what God was about to do.

On August 13, 1727, God sent a great revival to the community. Participants testified that this marked the coming of the Holy Spirit to Herrnhut. No longer were minor doctrinal differences debated. Love, forgiveness, and unity were experienced and there was a heightened dependence on God. "A prayer vigil was begun that continued around the clock, seven days a week, without interruption for more than one hundred years." (Tucker, p.71)

God had chosen his vessel, Zinzendorf. He had assembled a community of believers, and finally, He had prepared the Moravian community by sending the Holy Spirit on them in power. The final revelation of God's plan came several years after the great revival while Zinzendorf was attending the coronation of the Danish King Christian VI. There he met Anthony Ulrich, who was a Negro slave from the West Indies. Anthony had come to know the Lord and shared with Zinzendorf his desire that the gospel should be preached to his brothers. Zinzendorf immediately recognized this invitation from a negro slave as God's invitation to take the gospel overseas. This was God's invitation for Zinzendorf to be involved in His plan. In fact, God is always working around us. He is always speaking. The problem is that sometimes we do not recognize His voice. God speaks mainly to us today through His Word, the Holy Spirit, circumstances, and the church. Within a year, the first two Moravian missionaries had been commissioned to the Virgin Islands; thus, the Moravian mission movement was born.

The Moravian movement was one of the first, most effective and most enduring of all missionary enterprises ever undertaken. In just twenty years, they sent out more missionaries than all Protestants had sent out in the previous two centuries. One out of every ninety-two of their members became a missionary. If Southern Baptists in

America equaled the commitment of the Moravians, there would be 170,000 missionaries instead of 5,000, and Philippine Baptists would have 8,000 missionaries instead of approximately 40.

Zinzendorf himself served as a missionary in the Caribbean, but was primarily known and more effective as a missionary mobilizer. For thirty-three years he was overseer of a worldwide network of missionaries. His methods were simple and practical and have endured the test of time. All of his missionaries were lay people, not trained in theology, but trained as evangelists. They followed the example of the apostle Paul in that they were "tent-makers." The Moravians were self-supporting, working alongside their converts. Above all else, the Moravian missionaries were single-minded. They believed that people without Christ were lost, and they could never believe without a messenger speaking to them. They knew that messengers could never be sent without the great personal sacrifice of leaving goods and family for the sake of the gospel.

A testimony to the greatness of this movement is that Moravian missionaries spread the gospel across Europe, parts of Africa, the Caribbean, and to North, Central and South America. A testimony to the greatness of Zinzendorf can be summed up in his own words, "I have but one passion... 'tis He, 'tis only He." (Howard, p. 54)

WILLIAM CAREY
(1761-1834)

William Carey was an uneducated, poor English shoemaker. He was an unlikely candidate for greatness, especially greatness in the field of missions. In spite of this, Carey has been called the "Father of Modern Missions." His writings and life inspired a vision for missions on both sides of the Atlantic Ocean. During this time Christians believed that the Great Commission was given only to the Apostles; thus, relieving them of the responsibility of reaching the "heathen" with the gospel.

As a teenager, Carey was converted and became involved with a local group of Baptists. He devoted his leisure time to Bible study and lay ministries. Instead of following the path of his father as a weaver, he was apprenticed, at the age of sixteen, to a shoemaker and continued in this job until he was twenty-eight.

Carey spent many hours each day in the shop, perfecting his trade, but also growing in his relationship with the Lord. Like King David, these years of solitude and obscurity were used by the Lord to prepare Carey for "great things." He learned the importance of being faithful in the small things, and doing your best when given small assignments. The tedious job of repairing shoes must have also prepared him for the future when he would spend hours each day sitting at a desk translating the Bible. Also, while working in the shop, Carey began to familiarize himself with the world by reading books written by the great explorer, Captain Cook. Later, Carey said that the reading of Cook's voyages "was the first thing that engaged my mind to think of missions." (George, p. 20)

When Carey was 24, he became pastor of a small Baptist church, but continued to work in the cobbler shop. His study of Scripture and the collection of data concerning the population of nations and the religions began to take shape in the form of a booklet, which would later launch the modern mission movement. He came to believe that foreign missions was the central responsibility of the church. Furthermore, if you would have entered his shop during those days, you would have seen a large, homemade map suspended on the wall with facts about every country. "While engaged in making or mending shoes, his eye was often raised from his work to the map, and his mind was employed in traversing the different regions of the globe, and musing on the conditions of the various heathen tribes, and devising the means of evangelizing them." (George, p. 22)

Carey got in trouble one day when he challenged the ministers to give a reason why the Great Commission did not apply to them. They rebuked him saying, "Sit down young man, when God chooses to win the heathen, He will do it without your help or ours." (Tucker, p.115) The older ministers had quieted him that day, but they could not quench the fire that was burning in his heart. In the spring of 1792, he published the book, *An Enquiry Into the Obligation of Christians to Use Means for the Conversion of the Heathens.* In this eighty-seven-page book, Carey carefully examines the Great Commission and gives a brief history of early mission efforts beginning with the Apostles. He then presents page after page of world statistics to convince the reader of the great need in other lands. The fourth section of the book attempts to deflate the arguments dramatizing the impractibility of sending missionaries overseas. Last, Carey presents what is the Christian's duty in response to the call: prayer, giving, going.

After publishing the book, Carey was given the opportunity to speak to a group of ministers. He spoke from Isaiah 54:2, *"Enlarge the place of your tent, stretch your tent curtains wide, do not hold back; lengthen your cords, strengthen your stakes."* It is reported that he preached with great passion and concluded his sermon with the now famous challenge: "Expect great things. Attempt great things." (George, p.32) The meeting continued the next day with no apparent agenda concerning missions. When Carey saw that the meeting would be closed with nothing decided concerning the lost millions, he cried out, "Is there nothing again going to be done?" That was all it took! God had prepared the men's hearts for these words from God. As a result of this meeting, the first mission agency was formed.

The first missionaries appointed were John Thomas and William Carey. However, Carey had many barriers. His church said he had made a fast and foolish decision. His father called him crazy, and his wife refused to accompany him. Nevertheless, Carey continued to make plans to sail to India with one of the children and leave the rest of the family in England. However when time came to depart, Carey's wife, Dorothy, and her sister Kitty, reluctantly joined the missionary party.

Another surprise awaited them in India. The East India Company was in virtual control of the country and was opposed to mission work. Carey and his family did not have proper paperwork. There was the danger of being asked to leave the country. Carey moved with his family away from the city to be far away from the government officials. Furthermore, Thomas had spent not only his own money, but Carey's as well. Thomas had rented a big house with 12 hired servants. He also bought a very expensive vehicle. (George, p.97) Carey's family was now on their own.

The first several months were very hard for the family. They were adjusting to a new culture and trying to learn language. They were very poor. They were afraid of being sent back to England. There were also many different diseases. Furthermore, Dorothy and Kitty complained all the time. However, things improved when Carey was given the job as foreman of an indigo factory. They moved to a new place about three hundred miles from Calcutta. Carey and his family stayed there for several years, working and evangelizing. During this time their five-year-old son Peter died. This was too much for Dorothy. "She never did fully regain her mental faculties." (George, p. 117) In other words, she went crazy.

After seven years of ministry, Carey had not led his first Indian to Christ. Others may have given up and gone home, but Carey was convinced that "only God can open blinded eyes. Only God can convert lost sinners." (George, p. 99) "The conversion of one soul is worth the labor of a life." His faith surely kept him going during these early days.

In 1800, new missionaries arrived, and the team settled in Serampore, which became the center of Baptist missionary activity in India. Here, Carey would spend the remainder of his thirty-four years, and his mission team would become one of the most "famous missionary teams in history." The missionaries lived together and held everything in common. They met every Saturday night for prayer and for reaffirming these basic commitments to each other and to the Lord:

1. To set an infinite value on men's souls.
2. To acquaint ourselves with the traps which deceive the minds of the people.

3. To abstain from whatever deepens India's prejudice against the gospel.
4. To watch for every chance of doing the people good.
5. To preach "Christ crucified" as the only means of conversion.
6. To treat Indians always as our equals.
7. To cultivate their spiritual gifts, ever pressing upon them their missionary responsibility, since Indians can only win India for Christ.
8. To labor continually in biblical translation.
9. To give first priority to our personal Christian growth.
10. To give ourselves without reserve to the cause of preaching the gospel, "not counting even the clothes we wear our own."

This covenant was not taken lightly, but was lived out by all, especially Carey. His willingness to sacrifice material wealth and go beyond the call of duty became an example for all.

Carey never went back to England. He spent over forty years in service to the Lord in India. By the time of his death, he had translated the Bible and portions of the Bible into almost forty different languages. There were several thousand Indian converts. By 1817, Baptists missionaries had opened 103 schools with an average attendance of 6,703 pupils. (George, p. 145) Carey started a college, oversaw a team of researchers who translated many government projects into the local dialects. He wrote the first textbook on botany and developed one of the most magnificent gardens in all of India. He was also instrumental in stopping an Indian practice called *sati,* a ritual in which Hindu widows were burned alive with their dead husband. Carey's influence was not only felt in India, but also during the first 25 years after Carey sailed to India, a dozen mission agencies were formed on both sides of the Atlantic Ocean. The first American Board for Foreign Missions was formed as a direct result of Carey's *Enquiry* book and a five-student prayer meeting. More importantly, what arose from this student prayer meeting was the beginning of a student mission movement that has continued to this day.

Look and see what God can do! William Carey's life is a testimony to the greatness of God. His life is a challenge to anyone to expect great things from God and attempt great things for God. Two statements are a summary of Carey's secret to greatness. Late in life, he told his wife that if anyone should ever think to write anything about him that they should not say more than "I can work slow and steady. I can persevere in any definite pursuit. To this I owe everything." (Tucker, p. 114) Also at his own request, these words were written on his tombstone, "A wretched, poor, and helpless worm, on thy kind arms I fall." (George, p. 168)

ADONIRAM JUDSON
(1788-1850)

Adoniram Judson was the first American Baptist missionary who sailed for India in 1812, but because of God's providence, Judson instead served the Lord in Burma for nearly forty years. He became the most famous Protestant missionary in America during the nineteenth century. In fact, a survey conducted during that time revealed that he was the second most well known person in all of America! However, when the name Samuel Mills is mentioned, not many recognize him. Without the influence of Samuel Mills, Adoniram Judson may not have been sent as a missionary.

David Howard describes the beginning of the mission movement in America: "On the North American continent, the beginnings of overseas interest on the part of the church can be traced directly to student influence, and more precisely to the impact of one student, Samuel J. Mills, Jr. (1783-1818)." Born in Connecticut as the son of a congregational minister, Mills was brought up in a godly home. His mother reportedly said of him, "I have consecrated this child to the service of God as a missionary." This was a remarkable statement since missionary interest was practically unknown in the churches of that day and no channels (such as mission boards) for overseas service existed in America. "Mills was converted at the age of seventeen as a part of the Great Awakening that began in 1798 and touched his father's church. His commitment to world evangelism seemed to be an important part of his conversion experience. From the moment of conversion, on through the years of his study and for the rest of his public

ministry, he never lost sight of this purpose." (Howard, pp.
73-74)

"In 1806, Mills enrolled in Williams College, Massachusetts. This school had been greatly affected by the religious revival of those years, and devout students on campus had a deep concern for the spiritual welfare of their fellow students. Mills joined with them in their desire to help others. It was Mills' custom to spend Wednesday and Saturday afternoons in prayer with other students on the banks of the Hoosack River or in a valley near the college." In August 1806, Mills and four others were caught in a thunderstorm while returning from their usual meeting. Seeking shelter under a haystack, they waited out the storm and gave themselves to prayer. Their special focus of prayer that day was for the awakening of foreign missionary interest among students. Mills directed their discussion and prayer to their own missionary obligation. He challenged his companions with the words that later became a watchword for them, "We can do this if we will." (Howard, p.75)

"Bowed in prayer, these first American student volunteers for foreign missions willed that God should have their lives for service wherever he needed them, and in that self-dedication, really gave birth to the first student missionary society in America." Kenneth Scott Latourette, the foremost historian of church history, states, "It was from this haystack meeting that the foreign missionary movement of the churches of the United States began." (Howard, p.75)

Mills continued to meet with other students at Williams College who were interested in missions. In 1808, they formed the first student mission organization. In 1810, Mills, now a student at Andover College, met Judson, and together they started the first Foreign Missions Board. Mills never became a missionary, but continued to influence his generation as a missionary statesman, organizer and mobilizer. In 1818, while on a trip to Africa, Mills died at the age of thirty-five. Howard states, "Less than twelve years had passed since this amazing young man had knelt with his companions under the haystack near the Hoosack River. Yet in that short time he had formed a student missions society, helped start the first foreign mission board from North America, participated in sending the first missionaries, worked toward helping the poor in the slums of New York, helped start two Bible societies, ministered to the American native Indians of the Mississippi valley and finally died in an effort to stop slavery in America." (Howard, p. 80) He lived and died by the words, "we can do it if we will."

Adoniram's conversion is worth noting. He was raised in a Christian family, his father being a minister. At an early age, everyone knew that Judson was very smart. He knew Greek and Latin by the age of ten. He was very involved in church as a young teenager, even teaching Sunday school. However, while attending college he came under the influence of a young man by the name of Jacob Eames, who was an atheist, and Judson began to doubt even the existence of God.

Several years later, while traveling from New York, he stopped at an inn for the night. There was only one room remaining. No one wanted this room because next door, a young man was dying a horrible death. Nevertheless, Judson paid for the room but did not sleep very much. He was awakened several times by the moans of the dying man next door. In the morning he asked about the man. He was told that the man, Jacob Eames, had died during the night. Judson could not believe what he had heard! Judson was very sad. He rode down the road on his horse with the word, "lost," pounding in his ears. His friend was lost! He knew his friend had gone to hell! "Lost," "Death," "Hell"! His sleeping at that hotel could not be an accident! God had made himself known to Judson.

While on the mission field, the Judson's suffering, perseverance, and commitment are well recorded. Learning the Burmese language was the first test of their commitment. Missionaries, if they are to be effective, must spend time learning the language and culture of the people. "Adoniram struggled laboriously with the written language, which was a continual sequence of letters with no punctuation or capitals, and no divisions between word, sentences, or paragraphs." (Tucker, p.125) Besides the language, another barrier was that the Burmese people had no concept of an eternal God who cared for them personally. Their religion was Buddhism. Judson says, "Buddhism is a religion of ritual and idol worship. It is now two thousand years since Gaudama, their last deity, entered into his state of perfection; and though now he does not exist, they still worship a hair of his head, which is enshrined in an enormous pagoda, to which the Burmans go every eighth day." (Tucker, p.125)

The first few years of ministry, like the Carey's in India, brought little fruit. However, in their study of the culture, the Judson's discovered a way to reach out to the Burmese. This way was to build a *zayat,* which was a shelter open to anyone who wanted to rest, or to discuss the day's events, or listen to Buddhist lay teachers. Before building their *zayat,* the Judson's attended a religious meeting at a local *zayat* in order to know the customs and ways of the people. In just a month after they opened their *zayat* to the public, they had their first convert. Five years had now passed since coming to the mission field. The Judsons had taken the gospel and without compromise had explained it in a context

...rstand. Modern
mission... ...n.

...language and
culture... ...government.
Sometim... ...ed missi... ...naries to witness.
At other tim... ...persecuted Christians. In
1824, Judson a... ...were arrested and sent to a
death prison, whe... ...ted execution. "Life in the
death prison was ter... ...he missionaries were confined
with common criminals in a filthy, rat-infested, dark, wet
prison house, with chains binding their ankles. At night the
guards lifted the ankle chains to a pole suspended from the
ceiling, until only their heads and shoulders rested on the
ground." (Tucker, p. 128) This continued for a year, as almost
daily, Judson's wife Nancy, pleaded with officials to release
her husband. One cannot imagine the anguish and suffering
Nancy must have endured as she attempted to care for her
children during this long, difficult year. To make things
harder during this time, she also gave birth to a child.

Not long after Judson's release from prison, Nancy died.
Adoniram had already lost a child, so the death of his wife
was almost more than he could handle. Judson became
depressed. He was depressed for almost two years. "He
stopped talking with people and went into the jungle, where
he built himself a hut and lived there alone. He went so far
as to dig a grave where he kept vigil for days on end, filling
his mind with morbid thoughts of death. He was spiritually
empty and dry: 'God is to me the Great Unknown. I believe
in him, but I find him not.'" (Tucker, p. 129)

Judson recovered and returned from the jungle with a
new spiritual power and determination to complete what
the Lord had sent him there to do: evangelize and complete
the Burmese Bible. The remainder of Judson's years was

mixed with triumph and tragedy. More children died and a second wife, but God was faithful. The Burmese Bible was completed, along with a Burmese dictionary, and thousands of Burmese tribal people became believers. Maybe one reason that Judson persevered is because he never forgot the truth that God taught him as a young man; people without Christ are lost and without hope! When Judson was tempted to quit, he may have also remembered the words of his friend Samuel Mills, "we can do it if we will."

ROBERT MOFFAT
(1795-1883)

Today, the African continent has some of the most evangelized countries in the world. However, for years, Africa was known as the "graveyard for missionaries." Malaria and other tropical illnesses were feared more than savage tribes. It is hard to imagine today the sacrifice that early missionaries made as they said "goodbye" to their mother, father, brothers, and sisters. Many of them never went back to their home country or saw their family again. Sometimes it is easy to forget that many of the pioneer evangelists and missionaries suffered greatly.

Robert Moffat is no exception. He sacrificed greatly. He must not be forgotten. He and his wife Mary served in South Africa for over 50 years. They are one of the greatest missionary couples in modern history. Robert is known as the Father of South African missions. Moffat was born in Scotland in 1795. He was uneducated and did not go to Bible school. Nevertheless, he served effectively as an evangelist, a translator, an educator, a diplomat, and an explorer. He is more commonly recognized as being the father-in-law of David Livingstone.

Moffat grew up in a strict Presbyterian home, where his mother "gathered the children around her while she read stories of missionary heroes." (Tucker, p.141) At the time, Moffat didn't show much interest in spiritual things, but surely this type of upbringing laid a strong foundation for Moffat's mission career. Moffat was converted in 1814, while attending a Methodist church. The following year he heard a missionary message delivered by the director of the London Missionary Society (LMS). LMS was an interdenominational evangelical mission board, which at that time had missionaries all over the world.

Moffat having quit school after elementary was at first turned down by LMS as not being qualified, but after one year of study in theology with Rev. William Roby, the director of LMS, he was accepted and appointed. I am sure the mission board must have been pleased with his determination and his willingness to follow their policies of appointment. Young missionaries today should follow his example. If God has called, then the mission candidate should find out all he can about different sending agencies and their requirements. He should then be willing to make any sacrifice and adjustment in order to be appointed.

Moffat arrived in Cape Town in 1817. At first he was delayed. Other missionaries did not want him to leave the city. Moffat finally traveled hundreds of miles north to the Hottentot tribe. There he lived for over two years and was able to disciple a newly converted and infamous tribal chief. Moffat was like the apostle Paul, wanting to preach the gospel "to the regions beyond." He didn't want to build on what others had already started. That is the heart of the pioneer, going to unreached and hard to reach!

Two years after Moffat left England, Mary's parents finally gave her permission to go to South Africa. She arrived in December 1819, and three weeks later, she and Robert were married. Their "honeymoon" was a six hundred mile journey northeast to Kuruman through the hot and dry deserts, raging rivers, and dangerous forests. It was not a romantic honeymoon to say the least! However, this quick departure after their marriage and unity in their mission does show what qualities are necessary for a good missionary couple. I am sure Robert must have seen these good qualities in Mary before he left and that is why he wanted to marry her. The Scripture says, "that many are called but few are sent." There are many young men and women who have been called into service by the Lord, but have never seen what God could have done through them, because they married an unbeliever or someone who was unwilling to follow the Lord to the mission field.

The Moffats settled in Kuruman. This place became the model mission station through years of sacrifice and Moffats philosophy of the "Bible and plough." Moffat was definitely a pioneer in having a balanced approach of ministry. He preached the gospel and taught agriculture. Moffat also translated the Bible. It took Moffat twenty-nine years to translate the Bible. He was very happy when native men begin to grow in their faith, and even memorize God's word. This love for God's word was a great reward for all the years of toil and sacrifice.

Being a missionary is not easy. Learning a new language is hard. God wants the missionary to learn the language that the people speak in their home. This is called the heart language of the people. For the first ten years, Moffat communicated only through Cape Dutch, which was the trade language. The Bechuanans knew this language well enough for simple conversation, but could not understand the deep truths of the gospel. As a result, the Moffats saw little response to the gospel. After several weeks of intense study of the local dialect, they began to see immediate results; a religious awakening followed. Many were baptized and the first church was built.

After fifty-three years, the Moffats returned home to England. Robert continued for thirteen more years traveling throughout the British Isles. He challenged adults and young people alike about the tremendous needs of the mission field and the responsibility to take the gospel to lost nations.

Moffat died in August of 1883 at the age of eighty-eight. This epitaph was given to him, "Never had a truer hero been borne to the grave, nor one more thoroughly worthy of the name MAN."

DAVID LIVINGSTONE
(1813-1873)

David Livingstone left England in 1840 with the words of Robert Moffat ringing in his ears, "that sometimes seen, in the morning sun, the smoke of a thousand villages, where no missionary had ever been." (Tucker, p.151) These words were to set the direction for Livingstone's life. He was a missionary, a mobilizer, and even a national hero, but more than any of these things, he was a pioneer. He was a forerunner, like John the Baptizer, who, "*made the crooked ways straight, and the rough ways smooth.*" His ministry cannot be judged only by what he had accomplished at the time of his death, but what took place after.

Livingstone was born in 1813, in Scotland. His family was poor, but had a strong commitment to the Lord. To help with the family needs, Livingstone was forced to begin working fourteen hours a day when he was only ten years old. In spite of this hardship, he did not stop his education. With his first week's wages, he bought a Latin grammar book and enrolled in night classes. Many nights Livingstone studied by candle light way past midnight. After receiving Christ as his personal Savior when he was a teenager, Livingstone committed himself to foreign missions. He wanted to be a doctor and go to China, but because of family priorities, his education was continually delayed. In spite of these difficulties, Livingstone persevered, finally finishing his education at the age of twenty-seven.

Trials and hardships can either help us or hurt us. For Livingstone, these early trials only strengthened him for the latter, tough assignment the Lord would give him. Most would have given up the idea of finishing school, especially going to college and studying medicine; however the word "impossible" was not a part of his vocabulary.

In 1845, Livingstone was married to Robert Moffat's daughter and immediately left for a new assignment on the mission field. For the first few years of their marriage, they continually moved. Livingstone wanted to preach the gospel where no one had ever preached. He spent months away from his family. Sometimes his family went with him on his dangerous trips. Livingstone was criticized for not taking care of his family. In 1852, his wife and children returned to England and for the next five years, Livingstone continued his explorations without seeing his family or taking care of their needs. It is recorded that during this time, "his family was homeless and friendless, often living on the edge of poverty in cheap lodging." (Tucker, p.151)

"Free from family responsibility," he began his first and most famous expedition. Traveling from east to west, he followed the Zambezi River and made history by crossing the entire continent of Africa, arriving at the Coast. He returned to England and was welcomed as a hero. After only three days with his family, he launched a yearlong speaking tour. He amazed the crowds with his tales of horror and adventure. Standing before them with a maimed arm, surely he told the story of being attacked by a lion and surviving only because of his brave African companions. God began to capture the hearts of the British people for the terrible conditions of Africa, both physically and spiritually.

Two more explorations would give him a total of 29,000 miles of travel in Africa. Livingstone greatly increased the knowledge of the geography, fauna, and flora of the interior of Africa. He never forgot the greatest goals of his life, which were the putting down of the slave trade, and the evangelization of Africa.

Livingstone wrote much about the slave trade and was instrumental in getting it stopped. He describes their situations thusly: "Many of the party of slaves were children... two women had been shot the day before for attempting to escape... one woman had her infant's brains knocked out because she could not carry both it and her load." He continues, "The strangest disease I have seen in this country seems really to be broken-heartedness...speaking with many who died from it, they ascribed their only pain to the heart, and placed the hand correctly on the spot... Some slave owners expressed surprise to me that they should die, seeing they had plenty to eat and no work...it seems to be really broken hearts of which they die." (Worcester, p.74) Livingstone was so affected by the horrible slave situation that many times he was awakened from sleep, horrified by the things he had witnessed.

Livingstone also wrote much that stirred the hearts of young people to respond to the call of missions. He wrote, "God had only one Son, and He was a missionary and a physician." (Worcester, p.47) It is also recorded that as a young man, "he made a commitment that, as the salvation of men ought to be the chief aim of every Christian, he would give to the cause of missions all that he could earn beyond what was required for his subsistence." (Worcester, p.8) On his fifty-ninth birthday, these words were penned, "My Jesus, my King, my life, my all; I again dedicate my whole self to thee. Accept me, and grant, O gracious Father, that when this year is gone, I may finish my task." (Worcester, p.97)

In 1873, at the age of 60, his African servant found him dead, kneeling beside his bed. They loved their leader so much and could think of no better way to show him respect than by returning his body and papers to his associates at the coast. After burying his heart under a Mpunda tree, his body was dried in the hot African sun and then carried overland fifteen hundred miles to the coast.

After his death, there was an immediate response of new recruits. Henry Stanley, friend of Livingstone, picked up the exploration trail, making a 1,000- day journey through Africa. Missionaries followed wherever he went and the light of the gospel began to dispel the darkness. Livingstone never saw the results of his work, but he died, faithful, giving his whole heart and life to the African people.

J. HUDSON TAYLOR
(1832-1905)

Hudson Taylor, small in stature, but a giant in faith, still stands as one of the most influential Christian leaders since the Apostle Paul. His ministry lasted over a half of a century, and through his visionary leadership, inland China was opened to the gospel. At his death in 1905, there were over seven hundred fifty missionaries serving in the most remote places of inland China working alongside seven hundred Chinese workers. His sights were set on reaching the whole of China, all four hundred million people.

Taylor was born in 1832, in Barnsley, Yorkshire, England. His father was a Methodist minister. He raised all of the children in the strict Methodism of the day. He also was an evangelist and church planter.

His father was known to have a "heart for the villages close to their home that had no church." Sundays would find his father, "going from village to village preaching the Gospel." (Dr. & Mrs. Taylor, p.29) Before Hudson was born, being convicted by the verses in Exodus to "sanctify unto me all the firstborn... all the firstborn are mine," his parents asked the Lord to give their son, "the rich influence of the Holy Spirit and that their firstborn might be set apart." (Taylor, p.34) Pastors commonly visited their house where the children heard stories of faith and the needs of a lost world. At the age of four or five, Hudson was already talking about being a missionary when he was grown. (Taylor, p.37) In contrast to today's young people who see missions as some type of adventure, being a missionary was shown to be a life of sacrifice. An early quote from Taylor supports this. He prayed, "Lord Jesus, help us to be good brothers to you and to do some of your hard work in China and Africa." (Taylor, p.37)

At the age of seventeen, God made it clear to Hudson that he was to "spend his life" on the mission field. His call was clear and definite. He began to prepare immediately. (Taylor, p.86) Taylor began to read anything he could find on missions and was greatly influenced by the tales of Dr. Gutzlaff, who had served in the interior of China. Hudson made practical adjustments to his life to be a better-prepared instrument when the time came that he would go to China. He began to live a simpler life. He moved to an inexpensive boarding house so that he could give more of his money away to the poor.

Taylor also was careful to be faithful in the little things. He said, "A little thing is a little thing, but faithfulness in a little thing is a great thing." (Taylor, p.100) He began to spend more time alone with the Lord and to trust him for his daily needs, even experimenting or testing the faithfulness of God. His employer at that time was rather forgetful, but Hudson decided he would throw himself upon the Lord and not remind his employer about his pay. God would remind him, or he would go hungry. Every time, God proved Himself as a loving and caring father. These early baby steps of faith became the foundation of his faith-based mission organization. Hudson learned to, "move man through God by prayer alone." (Taylor, p.122)

Hudson arrived in China in 1853, and so began his long career as a missionary. His first six and half years were spent learning language, culture, and becoming immediately involved in ministry. Being useful, according to Hudson, included learning the language enough to preach, not just to get by. During this first period of his life, he studied two different dialects, and became convinced that in order to really relate to the Chinese people, he needed to adopt their dress and as much of their lifestyle as possible. He desired to move to the interior away from the protective ports, so as to be among the people. This move was very radical for that day and brought on him, "the anger of the European community, and even the ridicule and distancing of the missionaries from him." (Taylor, p. 320)

Hudson began to travel up the rivers and tributaries to cities and towns untouched by missionaries and unprotected by the government. These became known as his early evangelistic journeys. God used the Reverend William Burns to mentor Hudson on some of these journeys. Burns, even though in his latter years, would spend months at a time living on a boat going up and down the many tributaries preaching the gospel. Strategies used during those times were tract distribution, meeting the physical needs of the people through medicine, and following up on those who showed interest in the Gospel. It is noteworthy to mention statistics on one of these missions. On his sixth journey, they visited "fifty-eight cities, towns, and larger villages in twenty-five days." (Taylor, p. 293)

These foundational years provided many spiritual markers for Taylor's life. Practical experience, divine revelation, and providential leading were forming his strategy. He said, "As I looked upon the thousands of unreached and saw the darkness and sin of the interior, the comforts of Shanghai faded away." (Taylor, p. 286)

At the age of twenty-eight, with six and a half years of missionary experience, Hudson went back to Europe for his first furlough. He did not know what the future held. The next five years are known as the "Hidden Years."

God was working in Hudson's life. A plan was formulating for reaching the all of China. Hudson describes his crisis of belief after attending a worship service one night in England, "I was unable to bear the sight of hundreds of Christian people rejoicing in their own security while millions were perishing for lack of knowledge." (Steer, p.41) He went out to a solitary place to pray. He wanted to take twenty-two young people back with him but what if these young people went back to China with him and then starved to death? Would God be the same to them as He was to him? Would the supporters forget about them, as the people were saying? The result of this "wrestling with God" was the birthing of the China Inland Mission. (CIM) (Steer, p.41)

After meeting with the Lord on the beach and making the decision to go back to China no matter what the cost, whether to live or to die, a vision statement was proclaimed. Hudson said, "Our great desire and aim is to plant the standard of the cross in the eleven provinces of China hitherto unoccupied." (Steer, p.69) It was a simple statement, but it became the driving force of all efforts. Immediately they began to ask the Lord of the harvest for workers for each of the 11 provinces. They believed that God would call them out and He would provide for and sustain them. Some early guiding principles also give us insight into the direction and heartbeat of this new mission. These are listed as such:

1. We came out as God's children at God's command to do God's work.
2. We will wear native dress.
3. We will go inland.

Taylor began a movement that today is called Faith Missions. Missionaries called out to work with China Inland Mission would never solicit for money. His faith was like that of George Mueller, who cared for thousands of orphans by prayer alone. Taylor said, "There is a God, and He has spoken to us in the Bible, and He means what He says." (Steer, p.51) God could not fail. He would not abandon His children no matter where they lived. He could not forget His own. Just as a father cares for his children and is concerned daily that his children eat, there is a Heavenly Father who cares even more for His children. Psalm 84:11 became a theme verse of CIM missionaries. The Bible says, *"No good thing does he withhold from those whose walk is blameless."* Hudson also reasoned that if God could supply the needs of over three million Israelites in the desert for forty years, then if He sent three million to China, He could also supply their needs.

Prayer also characterized Taylor's life. From the calling out of workers to the strengthening of disciples, to the meeting of basic needs, prayer was the foundation of all he did. How did he make such an impact in his lifetime? Someone has said that Hudson Taylor burned with biblical conviction, and his tears flowed for the lost. He prayed for laborers and for the deepening of the spiritual life of the church. There were countless times over the fifty-year ministry of Hudson that he stood before a map, and stood with others, to ask God for the impossible. There was the asking of the "seventy," to which others said was impossible. God proved the skeptics wrong by giving the exact number and miraculously providing the resources for them. Then later, there was the asking God for one hundred, and finally late in his life, the Lord of the harvest was asked to send one thousand workers into the harvest field. Hudson Taylor's son said of his father, "He prayed about things as if everything depended on the praying, but he worked also, as if everything depended on the working. Someone observed in the early years that, 'The mission was formed by prayer, nourished by prayer and is still sustained by prayer month by month only in answer to believing prayer.' (Steer, p.71)

Taylor's ministry was characterized by going to the unreached. His desire was like that of the Apostle Paul to go "to the regions beyond." Probably one incident that helped shape this more than anything happened early in his ministry. While on one of his interior evangelistic journeys he met a cotton dealer. This dealer was the leader of a reformed Buddhist sect. The man came to Hudson after he heard him preach and said, "I have long searched for the truth, as my father had before me. I have traveled far, but I haven't found it. I have found no rest in Confucianism, Buddhism, or Daoism, but I do find rest in what I heard tonight. For now I believe in Jesus." He later asked Taylor, "How long has the gospel been known in England?" To which Mr. Taylor responded, "Oh several hundred years." The man said in response to this, "What! And you have now only come to preach the gospel to us? My father sought after the truth more than 20 years and died without finding it. Why didn't you come sooner?" (Steer, p.40)

Taylor was also never afraid to choose the hard road. Elisabeth Elliot, wife of martyred missionary Jim Elliot, has said that if you ever come to a crossroad in life and have a choice of an easy road or a hard road, always choose the hard road. That is the way the Master walked. His road always included a cross. He had, "no place to lay his head." Throughout his whole life, Mr. Taylor set the example of being willing to sacrifice. There were times of long evangelistic journeys. There were times of separation from family. The longest separation was for thirteen months. Even in his old age, he continued to travel and go to those who hadn't heard the gospel. He counseled the younger missionaries that they shouldn't be afraid of the cross or of the toil. They would be rewarded in full. He also said, "There is a needs be to give ourselves for the life of the world. An easy, non-self denying life will never be one of power. Fruit bearing involves cross bearing. There are not two Christs; an easy-going one for easy going Christians and a suffering, toiling one for exceptional believers. There is only one Christ." (H. Taylor) New candidates were told that, unless they were prepared to stand alone, separated from all, then they should never join the China Inland Mission.

After about twenty years on the field, Taylor went through a deep spiritual experience that some would call being "filled with the Spirit." Others call it "experiencing the deeper life." Taylor called it "The exchanged life." But before experiencing this great blessing, there were many days and weeks of inner struggle and dryness. He wrote in a letter one time, "My position becomes continually more and more responsible, and my need greater of special grace to fill it. But I have continually mourn that I follow at such a distance and learn so slowly to imitate my precious Master." (H. Taylor, p.153) He goes on to describe how much he struggled with temptation and how wicked his heart was. During this time he was praying that the Lord would make him more holy. There was a hungering and thirsting for more of God. The Holy Spirit was preparing Hudson for a deeper work and more fruitful work that did not depend upon his own strength and effort, but on abiding in Christ. When this "exchanged life" experience took hold of Hudson, he was never the same. He described himself as being a new man. He was a joyous man now as others recorded about him. "He was a bright happy Christian." (H. Taylor, p.157) Before, his work had been hard and toiling and burdened, now he was resting in Jesus. He was resting in his power. He had taken the yoke of Jesus upon him and had experienced that even in the midst of working hard, the yoke was light. It was said of him that whenever he spoke in meetings after that, a new power seemed to flow from him. Also, in the practical things of life, he had a new peace. Troubles did not worry him as before. He had learned in a new way to place all of his cares upon the Lord. He began to give more time to prayer. Instead of working longer, he began to go to bed earlier and rising earlier so as to give more time to Bible study and prayer. There was such a difference in his life that he could never stop telling others how they too might experience the Savior in this way. What is it that had taken place in his life? A letter from a friend is what impacted his life. In this letter it states, "Do you know, I now think that this striving, longing, hoping for better days to come is not the true way to holiness, happiness or usefulness. It is better, no doubt, far better than being satisfied with poor attainments, but not the best way after all." (Taylor, p. 155) This friend had read a book entitled, *Christ is All*. In this book the author explained that the finished work of Christ was not only payment for our salvation, but for our holiness and to only trust in him as our ever-present friend. Christ in you, the hope of glory. Galatians 2:20 put it this way, "*I have been crucified with Christ and I no longer live, but Christ lives in me.*" Hudson gave testimony that this sentence in the letter from his friend really changed his life. It states, "To let my loving Savior work in me His will, my becoming more holy is what I would live for by His grace. Abiding, not striving nor struggling; looking off unto Him; trusting him for present power; resting in the love of an Almighty Savior, in the joy of a complete salvation from all sin." (Taylor, p. 156) The truth of being one with the Savior became a new reality to him. He said, "It is a wonderful thing to be really one with a risen and exalted Savior, to be a member of Christ! Think what it involves. Can Christ be rich and I poor? Can your right hand be rich and your left poor? Or your head be well fed while your body starves?" (Steer, p.85) John 15 became reality to Taylor. He reasoned that in the root and in the stem, there is abundant fatness. These were all his.

At the end of Taylor's life, there were only thirteen thousand Chinese believers connected with their ministries, which is not too many after so many years of laboring. However he had laid the groundwork for a mighty move of God. Just thirty years after his death their numbers multiplied to over seven hundred thousand. Look what God can do through one man totally surrendered to Him!

CHARLOTTE (LOTTIE) DIGGS MOON
(1840-1912)

Lottie Moon was certainly not the first woman missionary, but she was one of the first well known female missionaries that inspired women to answer the call of God and do the work of an evangelist. She is the best-known Southern Baptist missionary. There is a yearly mission's offering named in her honor. There has been more money collected through this offering for missions than any other mission's offering in the history of the church. In 2003, over one hundred thirty million dollars was given by 45,000 churches to support over five thousand Southern Baptist Missionaries serving among 1,500 different people groups. There are many different kinds of baptists, and they all basically have the same doctrine. What makes Southern Baptists different from many groups is the way this denomination does missions. Southern Baptists cooperate to take the gospel around the world. There have been many problems, trials, and even controversies among the Southern Baptists, but the commitment to missions has been the one thing which has made the Southern Baptists the largest denomination in the world.

God promised Abraham that He would bless him, and in return Abraham was to become a blessing to the nations. There is a simple principle to be learned: if an individual, or church, or group of churches begins to have a desire to bring the gospel to the nations, God will bless them and help them.

Lottie Moon, in her life, and death, demonstrated this commitment to preach the gospel to the lost. As a result of this commitment, she has inspired thousands, if not millions to give not only their money, but also their lives in reaching the nations.

Lottie was born in 1840, into a rich family that owned a large tobacco plantation. Their house was located close to three presidential homes. She was one of seven children. All of her brothers and sisters became successful in their jobs. Education for women was fairly new in the deep South of nineteenth century America, so when Lottie graduated from Hollins Institute at the age of sixteen, she "was the best educated woman in the South." (Allen p.27)

After college she returned home to help run the plantation and later taught school in Danville, Kentucky. It was at Danville that God began to direct Lottie toward China. A Southern Baptist medical missionary to China was serving on the faculty of the school and Lottie, undoubtedly, had many opportunities to learn from him. In 1871, the Southern Baptists appointed the first single woman as a foreign missionary. When word of this spread, Lottie's sister, Eddie, volunteered, and was sent to China in 1872. Lottie, now thirty-three years old, followed one year later.

She established herself immediately as being capable of handling life as a missionary. She learned the language and was given responsibility in teaching and running a school for girls; something she was very qualified to do. However, she was not satisfied with this work. She wanted to be out among the millions who were perishing without Christ. Her first few years were "drudgery and plodding." Sometimes there is a false image of missionary life, in that, everything is always successful, easy, and exciting. Lottie experienced first hand the hardships and wrote extensively and honestly saying, "I really think a few more winters like the one just past would put an end to me. This is no joke, but dead earnest." (Tucker, p.235)

She wanted to do evangelism out in the villages, but the other missionaries would not allow her or any other woman to do this. Women were only allowed to be teachers. In meetings, and in letters, she was very outspoken saying, "Relegating women to such roles, she charged, was the greatest folly of modern mission." (Tucker, p.236) Such a view in her day was considered "radical," but permission was finally granted and she moved north to Pingtu. The trip was 120 miles, taking four days.

Pioneer evangelism was very difficult. Never had a Southern Baptist woman opened a new outpost in missions. Everywhere she went, the Chinese people called her "devil woman." She began her ministry by building relationships, by being a friend and neighbor. Everywhere she went she took her companion, Mrs. Chao. They began evangelizing with her family and their friends. This type of evangelism is called *oikos* evangelism. *Oikos* is a Greek word that means *household*. Paul preached to the jailer and he and his whole *oikos* were saved (Acts 16). Peter went to Cornelius' house and he had gathered all of his *oikos* to hear the gospel. It was not long until Lottie had many homes in which she could work. It was here in Pingtu that Lottie began to send letters home describing the conditions of the lost and the need for more missionaries, especially women.

As early as 1881, the Woman's Missionary Society at Cartersville had taken offerings for Miss Moon on Christmas Day. However, after hearing that the Methodists women had decided to observe the week before Christmas 1887 for prayer and self-denial for missions, Lottie passed on this idea to the Southern Baptists, and it was published in a mission's journal in December 1887. The first Christmas offering exceeded the goal by one thousand dollars and provided support for three new missionaries.

After four years of hard work in Pingtu, they saw their first baptism. Lottie had a policy of keeping "the movement as free from foreign interference as possible." It is probably because of this policy, that the church there grew steadily under the leadership of LiShou Ting, the Chinese pastor. Pingtu became the greatest evangelistic center in all of China. (Tucker, p.237)

Lottie left a legacy because of her love for lost people. On a typical day, she would visit at least two villages. She would teach Bible stories with pictures, and songs to the children. It is recorded that she visited as many as four hundred villages in one year.

Miss Moon is also remembered because of the many things she wrote. She challenged the home church to send out more money and workers. Once she wrote, "It is odd that a million Baptists of the South can furnish only three men for all China. Odd that with five hundred preachers in the state of Virginia, we must rely on a Presbyterian to fill a Baptist pulpit here in China." (Tucker, p.235) Another time she wrote saying, "Where is the silver and gold that should be in the Lord's treasury to send out those men and women who are asking to be sent to the lost? Alas! Alas! Some are adding more fields to their broad lands, some are laying up in banks, and some are spending on selfish indulgences. So these lost souls go down to death without ever hearing the name of Jesus. In the day of Judgment, at whose door will lay the sin." (source unknown)

Lottie's last legacy, which endeared her forever in the hearts of Southern Baptists, was the way in which she died. In 1911, wars, combined with plagues and famine, brought mass starvation to the area of Tengchow where Lottie was living. Her efforts at organizing a relief plan failed because of lack of funds from the United States. She continued to help as much as she could. She contributed from her own funds and personal savings, yet it was still a hopeless situation. Not being able to bear the burden anymore, she became depressed and refused to eat. A doctor was sent for, and only then, did they discover how close to death she was from starvation. In an effort to save her life, her colleagues made arrangements for her to return home, but their efforts were too late. She died en route, on board ship in the harbor of Kobe, Japan. She was seventy-two years old.

For years after her death, converts would stand and give their testimony: "When I was a child, I followed Old Lady Moon and learned hymns from her." Women in the village would ask, "When will the Heavenly Book Visitor come again?" The Chinese people who mourned for her did not talk about her education or ideas. They simply said, "How she loved us." (Allen, p. 289)

Look what God can do when one is totally surrendered to Him. Listen to Miss Moon's own prayer that she prayed as an old woman. "O that I could consecrate myself, soul and body to his service forever; O that I could give myself up to Him, so as never more to attempt to be my own or to have any will or affection improper for those conformed to Him." (source unknown)

AMY CARMICHAEL
(1867-1951)

"If it were possible to survey all the missionaries who have worked in all the world in all of Christian history, it would be seen that missionary work, most of the time, offers little that could be called glamour. What it does offer is a chance to die." (Elliot, p.176) A chance to pick up the cross and follow Christ, dying to self, ambitions, career, money, family, or like Amy Carmichael, even to the prospect of marriage. Carmichael was a true soldier for the Lord and also expected everyone else to be willing to sacrifice. She wrote, "Missionary work is a grain of sand, the work untouched is a pyramid.... Face it. Look and listen, alone with God. Then go, let go, help go, but never, never, never think that anything short of this is being interested in missions." (Elliot, p.94)

Amy Carmichael became as much of a legend and inspiration in England as Lottie Moon had become among Southern Baptists in America. She was a prolific writer, writing over thirty-five books and was fearless in the face of danger. Her character was beautiful and was the reason she had such a world impact. Carmichael embodied determination and perseverance, serving in India for fifty-five years without a furlough.

Amy was born in 1867 into a wealthy North Ireland family. Their four flourmills controlled much of local economy. Amy was sent to boarding school as a teenager and there, in her final year, "opened the door" to Christ. In spite of making a personal commitment to Christ at around fifteen years old, the decisive moment which determined the direction of her life did not come until two or three years later. One day, she and her siblings saw what they had never seen before, an old woman carrying a very heavy load. Amy and her brothers turned around, took the bundle, and helped her along by the arms. "This meant facing all the respectable people who were, like us, on their way home. It was an embarrassing moment. We were only two boys and a girl, and not at all committed Christians. We hated doing it. We were very embarrassed but we continued on, wet wind blowing us about, and blowing, too, the rags of the poor old woman." (Elliot, p. 31) As they continued down the street, "this mighty phrase was suddenly heard as it were through the rain: 'Gold, silver, precious stones, wood, hay, stubble— every man's work shall be made known; for the day will declare it, because it shall be declared with fire; and the fire shall try every man's work of what sort it is. If any man's work abide'—Amy turned to see who had spoken. There was nothing but the muddy street, and the people." (Elliot, p. 31) The children and adults continued on their way that day, but something had changed inside of Amy's heart. That afternoon she went to her room and stayed until she had surrendered everything to Him.

Amy began ministering to the lower class girls in town and had such success in winning them to Christ that some of the members of her church complained about "this unruly crowd." Numbers soon reached almost five hundred girls! Amy was a soul winner. During this time she had her "Macedonian Call" to missions while attending a missions Bible conference. It was as though she heard "the cry of the heathen," and could not stay home and do nothing about it. Amy was surely influenced at a meeting in 1887, where Hudson Taylor spoke of four thousand Chinese "passing through the gates of death everyday into darkness beyond— Savior-less, hopeless."

Amy was sent to Japan in 1892 at the age of twenty-four. Even though this was a very difficult experience for her, struggling with language, and finally having to leave because of "Japanese head," she learned one lesson she never forgot. One day while walking along the beach with one of the veteran missionaries, the missionary said, "You think all missionaries love one another?" That is exactly what she had thought. That is how it was supposed to be. God had commanded that Christians should love one another. How could the hardened hearts of the Japanese be broken with the power of the gospel, when Christ' own children could not love each other? (Elliot, pp.68-69) This experience caused her to pray, and to earnestly seek the Lord that He would enable her to love as He commanded us to love.

Arriving in India, she spent her first years in itinerant evangelism, working with a team among the lower class. This type of work was pioneer work, but not as glamorous or fruitful as a new missionary arriving on the field, hopes and prays for. "Again and again Amy's hopes were raised as one after another responded momentarily to the Gospel. Would the new convert have the courage to flee from home? If she did, what would happen? Would the missionary house be attacked?" (Elliot, p.142) Amy wrote, "I hope so! I should like to see some real fight." (Elliot, p.142)

On these evangelistic journeys, Amy began to hear and then see first hand the horrible practice of selling young girls and even babies to the Hindu temples to be raised as prostitutes. The terrible acts that went on in these temples were more than most missionaries would believe, and more than Amy could bear. She knew the stories were true. She began to pray that God would make a way to rescue these precious innocent souls from destruction. Their first answer, Preena, came in a most miraculous way. Amy records,

"Preena was a child of seven who lived in the temple house. Her father was dead. Her mother had been persuaded to devote her to the gods.

Once she managed to slip out and return to her mother, a twenty-mile walk to Tuticorin, one of the Sodoms of the province. The temple women traced her, and the mother, threatened her with the wrath of the gods, pulled the child's arms from around her neck and gave her back to them. They branded her hands with hot irons, effectively burning into her young mind the "horrible crime" of running away. "She had run away from a sacred calling." "One day Preena overheard a conversation about 'tying her to the god.' She imagined being bound with ropes to the idol in the dark rooms of the temple. She decided she would escape, no matter the cost. Like the other little girls, she was always being watched. She could think of only one way out. In desperation she went to the idol, threw herself down before it, and prayed that she might die." (Elliot, pp.167-168)

On the same evening that Amy's group reached the area, God sent an angel to the temple house. The angel took her by the hand, led her out, across the stream, through the woods. She was discovered by a Christian woman and taken to Amy. The child ran straight to Amy, climbed into her lap, and said, "My name is Pearl-eyes, and I want to stay here always. I have come to stay." (Elliot, p.167)

Within twelve years after she began this ministry of rescuing children, she had one hundred and thirty children under her care. In the decades that followed, hundreds of children, both boys and girls were rescued and raised at the Dohnavur Fellowship.

To have lived at the Dohnavur Fellowship during those years would have been to be under the teaching and influence of Amy. Through her books, we can still be inspired, challenged, and changed. We would have been challenged to win souls. She said, "O to be delivered from half-hearted missionaries! Don't come if you mean to turn aside for anything. Don't come if you haven't made up your mind to live for one thing—the winning of souls." (Elliot, p. 323)

If we would have been there during that time we would have heard these words, "We follow a stripped Savior. Those words go very deep. They touch everything—motives, purposes, decisions, everything." (Elliot, p. 304)

As a missionary candidate, we would have been asked these questions:

1. Do you truly desire to live the crucified life? (This may mean doing very humble things.)
2. Does the thought of sacrifice make you want to come or stay away?
3. Are you willing to do whatever helps most? That means a job that you may not be qualified for or what you came out to do.
4. Apart from the Bible, can you name three or four books which have really helped you?
5. Have you ever had the opportunity to prove our Lord's promise to supply your physical needs as well as Spiritual needs?
6. Do not come unless you can say to the Lord and to us, "The Cross is the attraction." (Elliot, p. 265)

Also as a missionary candidate you would have received these words of encouragement and challenge, "Dear, you are coming to a battlefield. You cannot spend too much time with him alone. You are soldiers and soldiers don't ask for ease or expect it. You are warriors, and when did warriors ask for an easy time? Or no wound? Or no heart-breaks?" (Elliot, p. 304)

We would have been taught simple truths concerning prayer:

1. We don't need to explain to our Father things that are known to Him.
2. We don't need to pressure Him, as if we had to deal with an unwilling God.
3. We don't need to suggest to Him what to do, for He himself knows what to do. (Elliot, p.365)

The ministry of Dohnavur Fellowship continues today. "Amy's children" can be found all over Indian serving the Lord. The fellowship continues to treat Hindu's, Muslims, as well as Christians through its hospital. Their goal is the same as it has always been; "We preach Jesus Christ as Lord, and ourselves as your servants for Jesus' sake." (Elliot, p.382) Look what God can do!

JIM ELLIOT (1927-1956)
AND OPERATION AUCA

In January 1956, five missionaries gave the ultimate sacrifice; they laid down their lives as martyrs trying to reach a "savage tribe" in the jungles of Ecuador with the gospel of Jesus Christ. This story made headlines across the world, and is still inspiring Christians wherever and whenever it is retold. The story of these five men and their mission has become the best-known Christian mission's story of the twentieth Century.

"O God, my heart is fixed," was a common prayer of Jim Elliot while in college, and this prayer tells the story of Jim's life and commitment. (Elliot, p.38) Even as a child, his heart was set on the Lord, "preaching to his friends in the front lawn." (Elliot, p.26) In high school he was never ashamed to let people know he was a Christian. He carried his Bible to school, prayed before meals, and witnessed to people, even if they didn't want to hear.

He loved the Lord enough as a teenager not to compromise, even in dating. In college, he made a commitment that he would not even kiss a girl until they were married. Love was not just a word, but also a serious commitment. He did not want anything or anyone to stand in the way of going to the mission field. He was "wary of women, fearing that they only intended to lure a man from his goals." (Elliot, p.31)

It might be thought from the above description that Jim was not fun to be around, but that is not so. He was handsome, athletic, and a natural leader. During his college days, he was a champion wrestler, and president of the

Student Foreign Missions Fellowship (SFMF). The SFMF, at that time, sent out more missionaries than any other time in the history of Wheaton College. Jim was a Greek major and an honor student, but spent at least an hour a day in personal quiet time with the Lord. He said, "I am seeking a degree in A.U.G., approved unto God." (Elliot, p.37)

It was sometime during the first two years of college that Jim made a commitment to become a missionary. This calling was not a mysterious thing to him, but was a direct response to the command of the Lord to go. Found in his journal, after his death, were statistics that he had written concerning the world's needs. The following is an excerpt: "1,700 languages have not a word of the Bible translated. Ninety percent of the people who volunteered for the mission field never get there. It takes more than a 'Lord, I'm willing!' Sixty-four percent of the world has never heard of Christ. 5000 people die every hour. The population of India equals that of North America, Africa, and South America combined. There is one Christian worker for every 50,000 people in foreign lands, while there is one Christian worker for every 500 in the United States." (Elliot, p.45)

In view of the clear command of Christ to go, along with these many facts of the needs for world evangelization, Jim believed that if he stayed in the United States, he would stand guilty before God on judgment day.

These statistics are not much different today. The needs today are just as great, and the command of the Lord has never changed. Any disciple of the Lord Jesus Christ must take seriously the command of the Lord to go and preach the gospel to every person in the world and to make disciples among every people group.

In 1952, Jim and his close friend Pete Flemming set sail for South America. They would join another college friend,

Ed McCully, who was already in Ecuador. Two other missionaries who would later become a part of "Operation Auca" were Roger Youderian, a World War II paratrooper, and Nate Saint, missionary pilot, working with Missionary Aviation Fellowship. Nate was the most experienced of all the missionaries, arriving in 1948, with his wife and small child. From 1952-1955, each of these missionaries was involved in separate ministries, some working with the Quichas of the high Andes Mountains, and the cannibal Jivaros. These five missionaries were from three different mission-sending agencies, and each one had plans to spend their entire lives as jungle missionaries. They would have probably had long successful careers as jungle missionaries, but God had another plan. This plan centered on the savage Aucas.

Operation Auca was begun in the fall of 1955. Nate Saint, on a routine flight carrying supplies to a missionary family, spotted a settlement of Auca Indians. Immediately, plans begin to be made on how to reach this hostile tribe. Since the 1500's, no outsider had ever been able to make a friendly contact with this tribe. The most recent killing had been ten years before, when eight employees of an oil company were speared to death.

This mission was "high adventure," and if successful would prove to be one of the greatest missionary breakthroughs in modern history. Just ten years before in the neighboring country of Peru, an Indian tribe there killed five missionaries. Jim and the others involved in "Operation Auca" studied every detail of the failed mission in Peru and did not want to make their fatal mistakes.

The team was sworn to secrecy, because they did not want reporters or even older missionaries to interfere with the plans underway. They developed a secret code for talking on the radio. With Nate Saint in the lead, they began to make routine trips over the Auca Village. Auca phrases, such as "we are your friends," were learned and shouted over a loud speaker as they flew over the village. Gifts were either dropped from the plane or lowered in a bucket from a rope. On one of their first tries, gifts were successfully exchanged; the Aucas had placed a live parrot, peanuts, and a smoked monkey tail in the bucket.

The team interpreted this as a sign of friendship. Some of the missionaries wanted to move quickly in making a personal contact. Some of the missionaries wanted to wait. Finally after much debate, they decided to go in as soon as possible. They were all aware of the dangers, but they were all, "ready to die for the salvation of the Aucas." (Tucker, p. 316) They were all praying that God would guide them in every dangerous step.

In December of 1955, they saw God's intervention and help. The Curaray River seemed to shrink back from its banks providing a beach airstrip to land the airplane. Normally at this time of year, the river was flooded. This beach was close enough for them to make contact with the Indians, but was far enough away to provide a way to escape.

On the night of January 2, no one slept much. There was a mixture of fear and excitement. Would this be the last time they saw their families? What would happen to them? Would the Indians treat them differently than all of the others who had tried to contact them? All of these thoughts and more entered their minds.

The plan called for Nate to make several trips on that first day. He would take the men and supplies onto the beach, that is, if he was able to land and take off. From the air, Nate was not sure if he could make a safe landing. He would not be able to know, until his plane touched down on the sand, then it might be too late. Nate recorded the first landing, "As we came in… we slipped down between the trees in a steep side slip… As the weight settled on the wheels I felt it was soft sand—too late to back out now. I hugged the stick back and waited. One softer spot and we'd been on our nose—maybe on our back. It never came." (Tucker, p.□17)

January 3 was a busy day on "Palm Beach." By nightfall, a tree house had been built, and all of the men were in place. It was decided beforehand, that every afternoon, Pete would fly out with Nate. January 4th and 5th were uneventful days. The men spent their time reading, praying, swimming, and trying to escape the many mosquitoes.

On Friday morning, January 6th, at 11:15 AM, three naked Aucas came out of the jungle. Jim waded across the river to meet them and a friendly exchange took place. There were two women and one man. The missionaries tried to communicate through actions and the few words that they had learned. The Aucas jabbered as if the missionaries understood their language. The Auca visitors stayed with them all day and then went back into the forest that night.

Saturday was another uneventful day. No visitors came back. The men were hopeful because of the contact they had made, but impatient with what would happen next. Jim talked about going to them, but wisdom prevailed and he stayed at Palm Beach. Ed wrote to his wife that much discussion had taken place about trying to go to the Auca village as soon as possible to build an airstrip. With Nate and Pete flying out every night, the wives knew what was happening and the men were supplied with fresh food and supplies daily.

On Sunday morning, the team enjoyed ice cream and blueberry muffins that had been sent. In the afternoon, it was agreed upon that a visit should be made to the Auca village. At 12:30 PM, Nate reported to his wife on the radio that ten men had been spotted "en route" to Palm Beach. "Looks like they'll be here for the early afternoon service. Pray for us. This is the day! Will contact you next at four-thirty." (Elliot, p.194)

At four-thirty, the radio was silent. "Maybe the radio is not working, or they are busy entertaining the visitors," thought Nate's wife. However as the time ticked by and nighttime fell in the jungle with no word from the missionaries, the reality of the situation began to be realized. The secrecy of the mission was not broken until the morning of January 9th. Another missionary pilot was sent to Palm Beach, and reported that the plane had been destroyed and there was no sign of the men.

All five were brutally killed with spears! All five were under 35 years old. Five wives were left without husbands, and 9 children were now fatherless. They had not only been willing to live their lives as a living sacrifice for the Lord, but they had been willing to lay down their lives for the sake of the gospel and the salvation of a few hundred Aucas.

They never personally got to witness to the Auca Indians. They never got to preach a sermon to them or sing songs in their language. They had only been involved in Operation Auca for less than 6 months, but they had been obedient! They had done what the Lord told them to do. They had loved a small group of "savage Indians" that most did not know or care about.

Two years later, Elisabeth Elliot, wife of Jim, along with Rachel Saint, sister of Nate, were invited to come and live among the Aucas and they obeyed. They were willing to love the very ones who murdered their family members. Many of the Aucas have now become believers. The very ones who killed the men became leaders in the church. Jim's daughter was baptized by one of the men who killed her daddy.

During his college years, Jim had prayed that his life would be an offering poured out to the Lord. God answered his prayer. Look what God can do through one life totally surrendered to him.

DOUG AND EVELYN KNAPP
(1927-, 1930-)

An African proverb says, *"Haba na haba hujaza kibaba"* (Drop by drop the bucket fills). (Knapp, p. 21) It's a simple but profound concept. Slow steady drops do fill a bucket. In Philippine context the equivalent would be *"Hinay hinay basta kanunay."* Slowly but surely God's blessings filled the Kyela District of the East African country of Tanzania through the Knapp's twenty-six year ministry.

Doug was an ordained deacon who served faithfully in his local church in Florida, U.S.A. For several years he served as an agriculture extentionist with the local government, and then began writing a weekly column for the *Miami News*. This publicity led Doug to a successful career in television. He became host to a daily program called "City Farmer." "City Farmer" became the top-rated local morning show in their city. However, God had other plans for the Knapps.

What an adjustment it must have been to go from the lights of a television studio to living in the "bush country" of Eastern Africa, where there were no lights at all. God's call to follow has never changed. When God called Abraham he called him to leave his land and family and go. When Jesus called the first disciples, they left their boats and their father. You cannot stay where you are and go with God the same time. A choice has to be made. Doug and Evelyn Knapp made the choice, left all that they knew and followed Christ to the Nyakyusa people. Their assignment was to evangelize two hundred and fifty thousand people. When they arrived in 1964, there were a few believers, but the majority were pagans and animists.

Doug recounts the beginning of their work: "A pair of eyes looked out from behind an ancient baobab tree, watching every move Evelyn and I made. That lone, gnarled, bubous tree, which gave the illusion it grew upside down with roots pointing skyward, created a strange contrast to the rest of the scene. Africans say God planted baobabs right side up, but *Shetani* (Satan) came during the night, uprooted them, and stuck them back in the ground upside down. Baobabs are common to the other areas of Tanzania but not to the Kyela District. Somehow this single tree had taken root there. But the attitude of the man hiding behind the tree was common in those days as we began our work there. *Hujambo, habari, Bwana?* (Hello, how are things, Mr?), I called in greeting, starting toward him.

Suddenly, with the seeming speed of the graceful gazelles, which bound across the vast stretches of Africa, he fled into the banana grove. I dropped my outstretched hand, kicked my foot in the dirt, and tore up a banana leaf in frustration.

We were trying to get something started in the Kyela, but we couldn't even get close to them. They were afraid of us. White faces were not uncommon in those days, so we were very confused at the apparent fear of the people. They ran when we approached them in the marketplace and when we approached their thatched, bamboo-and-mud-huts and called out *"Hodi"* (May I come in?), they would hide or run out of the back door.

Finally I gathered some African men we'd brought down from Tukuyo to help start our demonstration *shamba* (farm) and said, 'Go out among the people and find out what the problem is.'

'They're afraid of you Bwana Nepu,' the men told me when they returned. 'The *mchawi* (witchdoctor) told them you have come to take their blood. He told them you want to use their blood to mix black magic potions in order to make yourself more powerful.'

This great barrier was slowly overcome as the Nyakyusa began to observe the fast-growing corn on the demonstration farm. There eyes began to get bigger and bigger the more they looked. They could also see that the cows had big bags of milk and that the chickens and eggs were big. Eventually they began to ask questions, and one man even requested seeds, but he was afraid to come and get them. Doug says, "I wanted to rush up, take him by the hand, and tell him I'd come to be his friend, but African patience had begun to teach me a lesson. Laying the packet of corn seeds carefully on the ground, I backed away. 'Take this,' I said. 'I'll be glad to help you if you have any problems planting them. There are some special things you can do to make the soil better for crops.'

Taking another step back, I added, 'Come back tomorrow, and I will give you more.' He picked up the seeds and ran off. Suddenly, he realized he had violated African politeness and failed to say thank you. '*Asante sana, Bwana,*' he called with a wave as he disappeared into the brush. 'Thank you very much also, Bwana,' I responded under my breath, 'for coming near enough to talk.' (Knapp, pp.163-165)

This was the breakthrough they had been praying for. The bucket began to fill and the Knapps began to have opportunity to share their knowledge about farming. More importantly, they began to have opportunity to share about Christ' love and salvation. After sharing the gospel with an elderly gentleman, the man asked Doug, "When was it that God sent his son Jesus to save us?" "It was a long time ago, almost two thousand years," Doug responded. "Why did it take so long for you to come and tell me about it?" he asked in amazement. "If only I had heard about this when I was a boy...it would have made a great difference in my life." (Knapp, p.181)

Over the next twenty years, church growth was steady. Churches were started, disciples were trained, and God called out leaders. In fact, slowly but surely churches began to be started all over the valley. Jesus was building his church just as He said he would. The gospel had been sown abundantly and the Knapps began to be burdened that they were not reaping, as they should. There should be more fruit for the labor that had taken place. At that time there were around eighty churches with an average attendance of thirty or forty members each.

To help bring in the harvest, God led the Knapps to begin a partnership with many American volunteers. Once every two years, these volunteers partnered with nationals in conducting *jitihada* (crusades), all over the Kyela District. The spiritual breakthrough they had prayed for since 1964 finally came during a 1982 crusade. While driving to a crusade preaching point, a crowd stopped the vehicle in which the team was riding and asked them to come to their village, because they had two people who were very sick. The interpreters explained to the crowd that there were no doctors and no medicine. However, the crowd insisted that they come anyway.

"Please, come help," they said. "These people are very sick, and they will die if you don't come help us."

"I will come and pray for them," said one volunteer.

They followed the interpreter and guide to the village and made their way to a little hut. A man lay inside, showing no signs of life. Relatives, expecting him to die, were already gathering for the funeral. The volunteer fell on his knees, prayed for the man and then went to another hut and prayed for a man with pneumonia, then they immediately left and went to the outdoor preaching service. A loud commotion interrupted the service several minutes after the preaching had begun. A large number of people joined the crowd. Looking out over the crowd the volunteer recognized the man as the one he had prayed for. God had done a miracle. The crowd was totally amazed!

As word spread, large numbers of people started attending the services and more people began to be healed. It was just like the book of Acts. Cripples were healed, the blind saw, and the deaf heard. Crowds of one hundred and more began gathering on the side of the road. They would stop the preachers as they were going to another area, and ask, "How can we be saved?" In three weeks, over eight thousand received Christ. Average church attendance went from thirty to over one hundred. One church, in a small village grew to over five hundred members!

From 1964 until 1984, eighty churches were planted. When the Knapps retired in 1989, there were over four hundred churches among the Nyukyusa people. There were 33,775 total baptisms between 1978 and 1986.

No one can take any credit for what has taken place in this valley. God has sent an awakening. However, there are some observations that can be made from the Knapp's ministry which can encourage us and help us. What did they do?

1. They stayed a long time. They were willing to persevere. What if they would have left after five years or ten years or even fifteen years? They would not have seen the harvest.
2. They had a ministry of assistance. They loved people and tried to help them physically.

3. They loved and trained their pastors.
4. They emphasized church planting and church development. They planted churches within walking distance of every person.
5. They used national evangelists.
6. They developed youth and women's programs.
7. They conducted regular evangelistic crusades.
8. They used many volunteers.
9. They helped with church construction. They partnered with the local churches in helping them build permanent buildings.
10. They preached and ministered in the schools.

Look and see what God can do through a deacon and his wife who are willing to leave what they have and go anywhere and do anything for the sake of the gospel!

GEORGE MUELLER
(1805-1898)

Every so often, there is a man or woman who is willing to stand on the promises of God and believe God in spite of impossible circumstances. Abraham believed God when he was old and it was impossible for his wife Sarah to have children. Elijah believed God and was provided for by birds and a very poor widow. Peter believed Jesus, went fishing, and found a coin in the mouth of a fish, just as Jesus said he would. George Mueller dared to trust God for the needs of countless orphans.

Today, he is still remembered as one who had great faith. However, if George Mueller could still speak to us today, he would probably say, "God is not looking for big faith, but even a little faith in a big God." George Mueller came to know God in such a personal way, that he trusted him completely.

Mueller was born in Germany in the early 1800's into the Lutheran denomination. During that time, the Lutheran church was not as spiritually alive as it had been during the Protestant Reformation in the 1500's. George was a rebellious young person, often in trouble with his father, and with the police. Once when he was sixteen, he spent a whole month in jail!

At nineteen, George was accepted into the University of Halle, to begin his studies to become a Lutheran Minister. At this point in his life, George was not even converted. He was one of the regular attendees of the beer house located across the road from the campus. He had the reputation of gambling more than he read his Bible.

George's life changed in the fall of his second year of college. He was invited to a home Bible study. At the home

Bible study, he realized that he had known the facts of Jesus' death, but to him, "God had never really lived." (Bailey, p. 19) Mueller wanted to become a true believer because of the example of the Bible study leader. Back in his room, George cried out to God, "At last! God, tonight I am yours!" (Bailey, p. 20)

In the weeks that followed, George committed himself to becoming a missionary. This would mean living a life of faith, instead of ease in one of the established Lutheran churches. When George told his father about his decision, his father was angry and refused to give George "permission" to become a missionary. However, George's heart was set, and he chose to follow the Lord's command to "leave all to follow him." This decision required a great step of faith, because in making his decision to become a missionary, his father refused to give him any more money for school. George would have to trust the Lord for everything: his tuition, room, food, etc. This first step of faith would set the direction for his life and ministry.

Back at school the next week, with no money, and no means to make money, George prayed, "God, you know exactly what I've done and what this means. You know what I need... Money for rent, food, etc. I'm depending on You, God, to see that I get it. In your time. In your way. I'll wait." (Bailey, p. 33) This was the first of many thousands of prayers George prayed, and God was faithful. Not long after he prayed, there was a knock on the door. An American professor had come by to see if George would be willing to tutor him and three others in German. They would be willing to pay! George could not believe it! It would be just enough to cover his expenses!

God also provided for George a free room in a local orphanage, and it was the story of how this orphanage was started that amazed George the most. Over one hundred years before, A. H. Franke, a theology professor, had no money, no wealthy family, but had built an orphanage for over 2,000 children through prayer alone.

George arrived in London in 1830 as a missionary to the Jews, and later served as a pastor. It was in London that Mueller saw the terrible conditions of "almhouses," which were government run orphanages. While praying about what should be done, he miraculously came across a biography about A. H. Franke. God was speaking to George! There could be no other explanation. God was leading him to begin an orphanage.

This orphanage would be for the children of course, but there was more. George said, "But I know you can reach up and touch God when you pray. I've proved it to myself. It changed my life. And I want to convince other people. I think I can, if I can point to something God has done through prayer. Something real and tangible. If God can take me, a very poor man; if I can bring together twenty children in an orphanage; if He will give the strength to ask no man for anything—to ask only Him for my money—then I will prove to some people anyway that God is still faithful today." (Bailey, p. 85)

This is what George Mueller did. He prayed! He never asked man for anything! He placed himself on the altar of God in 1835. God was faithful. God never failed. God was always right on time. Many times they had no money at all, and God provided for them literally, hour by hour. One time, the children sat down to breakfast, but had no food. They prayed, thanking God. While they were praying, there was a knock on the door. A wagon delivering bread had broken a wheel, and the owner wanted to know if the orphanage needed any food. This miracle was one of the many that are recorded as testimony to God's faithfulness.

By 1870, George was caring for over 2,000 orphans, living in five different homes. These homes were not just places to live, but they were monuments. Living monuments that God is alive and answers prayers. He is the same yesterday, today, and forever. He is willing to use anyone, even poor people, who are willing to trust him.

George, at the age of seventy-two, began traveling all over the world preaching and giving testimony of God's faithfulness. He traveled to 42 countries and traveled over 200,000 miles! Look what God can do with one who is totally surrendered to Him!

THIRD WORLD MISSIONS

Great missionaries in this modern era of missions (1792-present) have mainly been from Europe and America. However, with the growth of the church in third world countries, God is raising up missionaries from many nations to finish the task of evangelizing every tribe in the world.

These "receiving countries" are now becoming sending countries. South Korea is a good example. One hundred years ago, less than 1% of Korea's population was evangelical. Now with an evangelical population of 30-40% they are sending missionaries all over the world, especially to work among Muslim people groups.

God's plan from the beginning has been that those who are blessed should then become a blessing to other nations. By 1980, the Third World was sending out and supporting more than ten thousand cross-cultural missionaries.

In 1982 the count was more accurately determined to be fifteen thousand. Presently, there are more cross-cultural missionaries from third world countries than from western countries. God is waiting and the world is waiting for third world Christians who are surrendered to Him and willing to believe and trust God.

In fact, the world has already seen a few of these Christians from Third World countries who were willing to be used and who have impacted thousands and even millions with the gospel.

One of these Christians is Rochunga (Ro) Pudaite. He was born in the Indian village of Senvon, not far from the Burmese border. Senvon was so remote that it was not even listed on the census and had no government schools or post office until Ro, as a young man, brought the matter before the government officials.

Ro's father, Chawnga, was an uneducated, but very effective pioneer evangelist. After hearing the gospel, he walked over 160 kilometers to the house of a missionary. There, he learned to read and study the Bible. After this, Chawnga returned to his people, the Hmar tribe, and for fifty years spent his life going from village to village evangelizing. As a result, over 80% of the Hmar tribe is now born-again.

When Ro was only ten years old, his father spoke to him about the great need for a Hmar Christian to obtain further education so that he could translate the Bible into the language of his own people. Chawnga had his son, Ro, in mind.

How could a boy from such a remote place and from such a poor family ever receive an education? There were many obstacles! As a young teenager, Ro walked for six days through the jungle to attend boarding school! He taught himself English, finished high school, and was given a scholarship to attend Bible school in Scotland. There he met the famous evangelist Billy Graham. He then finished his schooling at Wheaton Bible College in America.

Ro translated the Bible into the Hmar language, and then became leader of the Indo-Burma Pioneer Mission Organization. By the 1970's this mission had started 65 village schools, a high school, a hospital, and had 350 national missionaries. Ro has now become founder and president of *Bibles for the World,* with a vision of sending a Bible to the world's 500,000,000 telephone subscribers.

Festo Kivengere is another great Third World Christian of the 20th century. Converted at the age of ten as a result of a great revival in East Africa, he was used of God in bringing thousands to Christ both in Uganda and Tanzania. In one year alone, Bishop Festo reported over 30,000 conversions! As Bishop of the Anglican Church in Uganda, he was also a voice of hope during the dictatorship of Idi Amin, who murdered over 500,000 people from 1973 to 1981.

Festo escaped Uganda in 1977 and as an exile spoke out boldly against the regime of Idi Amin. Two years later, he returned and began helping the country rebuild itself.

Festo was heavily involved in relief work, but his main priority was the spiritual welfare of the people. Because of Festo's influence, "The church is the only institution which has come out of the Amin era strengthened and fortified rather than weakened, and it has become a key factor in reconstruction and rehabilitation of the nation as a whole." (Tucker, p.449)

Luis Palau, a Brazilian, is another Third World Christian that God is using. He has become one of the most effective missionary-evangelists in the world today. Philip Teng is another. He served as a missionary in Malaysia and later traveled all over the world preaching the gospel and challenging Asians to take the gospel to other nations and peoples.

There are many more unnamed missionaries from Third World countries, even from the Philippines. God's call has not changed. He has commanded His children to take the gospel to every person in the world. He has commanded his children to make disciples among every language group. This call has no conditions! There is not one call for the American and one for the Asian. There is not one call for the poor and one for the rich. The God of all the nations calls disciples from any nation to take the gospel to all nations. Are you ready? Are you willing? The world will see what God can do through you, if you are willing to surrender to Him 100%.

BIBLIOGRAPHY

Allen, Catherine. *The New Lottie Moon Story*. Nashville, TN: Broadman Press, 1980.

Bailey, Faith Coxe. *George Mueller.* Chicago, IL: Moody Press, 1958.

Elliot, Elisabeth. *A Chance to Die: The Life and Legacy of Amy Carmichael.* Grand Rapids, MI: Fleming H. Revell, 1987.

Elliot, Elisabeth. *Shadow of the Almighty.* San Francisco, CA: Harpers, 1988.

Elliot, Elisabeth. *Through Gates of Splendor.* Wheaton, IL: Tyndale House Publishers, 1981.

George, Timothy. *Faithful Witness: The Life and Mission of William Carey.* Birmingham, AL: New Hope, 1991.

Howard, David. *Student Power in World Missions.* Downer's Grove, IL: InterVarsity Press, 1979.

Knapp, Doug and Evelyn. *Thunder in the Valley.* Nashville, TN: Broadman Press, 1986.

Steer, Roger. *Hudson Taylor: Lessons in Discipleship.* Finland: Monarch Publications, 1995.

Taylor, Dr. and Mrs. Howard. *Hudson Taylor: In Early Year: The Growth of a Soul.* Great Britain: R & R Clark, Ltd., 1911.

Taylor, Dr. and Mrs. Howard Hudson. Hudson Taylor's *Spiritual Secret.* Chicago, IL: Moody Press, 1987.

Tucker, Ruth A. *From Jerusalem to Irian Jaya.* Grand Rapids, MI: Academic Books, 1983.

Worcester, Mrs. J. H. *The Life of David Livingstone.* Chicago, IL: Moody Press, 1975